Original title:
The Idea Of You

Copyright © 2024 Book Fairy Publishing
All rights reserved.

Editor: Theodor Taimla
Author: Samira Siil
ISBN HARDBACK: 978-9916-759-12-7
ISBN PAPERBACK: 978-9916-759-13-4

Unseen Radiance

Beneath the veil of twilight's cloak,
Glistens love without a word,
In the silence, truths evoke,
A luminous path unheard.

Through the mist where shadows tread,
Whispers of the unseen guide,
Glimmers of a sun not shed,
Hidden light where fears reside.

In the unseen, find the glow,
Stars align with silent prayer,
Radiance in the ebb and flow,
Grace within, beyond compare.

Canvas of Emotions

Brushstrokes weave a tale untold,
Hues of laughter, shades of pain,
Every stroke a fragment bold,
Of a heart's unending rain.

Colors merge in fervent dance,
Passions play in vivid lines,
A symphony of deep romance,
Woven into life's designs.

Each emotion, pure and bright,
On the canvas, stories blend,
In the art of love and plight,
Eternal truths, their journey send.

Fleeting Captures

Moments pass like morning dew,
Ephemeral as the dawn,
Glimpses sweet, of life anew,
Before the breath is gone.

Eyes that meet in silent grace,
Smiles that linger in the dusk,
Memories time can't erase,
In the heart forever hushed.

Cherish now, the fleeting touch,
Epics told in whispers brief,
In the dance of time as such,
Find the joy, beneath the grief.

Quiet Presence

In the hush of morning light,
Whispers dance upon the air.
Silent shadows taking flight,
Leaving traces here and there.

Beneath the sky, so vast and blue,
Softly tread, the world unfolds.
In this calm, I find anew,
Stories that the silence holds.

Gentle rustle of the leaves,
Echoes of a time so still.
Nature's breath as it believes,
Whispers of a quiet thrill.

Subconscious Longing

In dreams we weave a silent song,
Threads of thought that linger deep.
Yearning hearts where we belong,
In the silent watch of sleep.

Beneath the surface, shadows play,
Hints of feelings yet to bloom.
In the night and through the day,
Subtle whispers in the room.

Across the void, our souls entwine,
Murmured hopes and secret fears.
Silent wishes, softly pine,
In the dance of distant years.

Invisible Ties

Threads unseen but deeply known,
Bind our hearts in gentle grace.
Silent bonds, forever sown,
In life's ever-changing embrace.

Eyes that meet and softly glance,
Words unspoken, understood.
Within this silent, knowing dance,
Lies a bond of brotherhood.

In the folds of time we drift,
Connected by these unseen lines.
Through the storms and through the lift,
Soul to soul, the heart aligns.

Faint Silhouettes

Shadows waltz in twilight's glow,
Faint reflections of the past.
Echoes of what we once did know,
Moments lost, forever cast.

Through the mists of time we see,
Figures soft in dusk's embrace.
Silent ghosts of you and me,
In this half-lit, gentle space.

Whispers in the pale moonlight,
Stories etched in silhouette.
In the stillness of the night,
We remember, we forget.

Exquisite Threads

In the loom of time, threads interlace,
Moments woven with tender grace.
Colors merge, creating art so vast,
In the tapestry of life, we're cast.

Each thread a story, spun with care,
Patterns emerging, beyond compare.
From whispers of love, to cries so grand,
We weave our souls with gentle hand.

Golden hues of dawn, twilight's kiss,
In the woven essence, purest bliss.
Threads of joy, and sorrows tight,
Intersect in the cloak of night.

Textures rich, in life's embrace,
Every strand finds its place.
Bound by fate, yet free in dance,
In every thread, we take our chance.

Unchained Moments

Seize the moment, let it fly,
An unchained bird in the open sky.
Wings of freedom, flutter and soar,
In each breath, life's distant shore.

Capture joy in fleeting frames,
Unraveled moments, break the chains.
Time's no master, ever free,
In whispers of eternity.

Glimmers of light in shadows found,
Moments drift without a sound.
Echoes resonate within our souls,
As unchained moments make us whole.

Embrace the now, let it unfold,
In every heartbeat, stories told.
In the tapestry of endless time,
Moments unchained, pure and sublime.

Hidden Dreams

In the quiet of the midnight hour,
Lie hidden dreams, with subtle power.
Whispers soft, like wind's gentle breeze,
In secret realms, they find their ease.

Visions dance in shadowed light,
Silent hopes take quiet flight.
Stars above, in whispers gleam,
Guiding paths to every dream.

Locked away, yet ever near,
Hidden dreams confront our fear.
Behind veils of the night's embrace,
Find their truth in time and space.

Unveil the heart, let dreams be free,
In the calm of night's decree.
Hidden dreams, our souls' sweet plea,
Charting courses, destiny's key.

Ethereal Echoes

Softly whispers the moonlit night,
   Stars amidst their silver flight.
Cosmic dreams on wings take flight,
   Ethereal echoes, silent might.

Shadows dance on the edge of sight,
   Galaxies merge in dim twilight.
Celestial bodies in gentle fight,
   Ethereal echoes, pure delight.

Veiled in mist, the hidden bright,
Kaleidoscopic hues, a dazzling sight.
   Unseen forces, ever so slight,
Ethereal echoes, gleaming light.

In the vast and endless height,
Mysteries whisper, hearts ignite.
Eternal secrets, day and night,
Ethereal echoes, infinite in plight.

Whispers of Existence

In the stillness of dawn's first glow,
Silent murmurs begin to flow.
Life's quiet hum, a gentle show,
Whispers of existence, soft and slow.

Beneath the stars in moon's warm hue,
Silent prayers in the night accrue.
Invisible hands guide and construe,
Whispers of existence, pure and true.

From ancient trees to river's edge,
Nature's symphony, a living pledge.
In silent leaves, a sacred wedge,
Whispers of existence, on the hedge.

Through the fabric of time's own thread,
Silent footsteps where souls have tread.
In unseen realms where dreams are led,
Whispers of existence, softly spread.

Mirage of Our Souls

In the desert's endless reach,
Furtive phantoms softly breach.
Visions shimmer, truth and preach,
Mirage of our souls, they beseech.

Through the sands of time's vast tread,
Whispers of the past are spread.
Echoes of what once was said,
Mirage of our souls, still ahead.

Reflections in the heat's embrace,
Glimmering forms we cannot trace.
Yearning hearts in endless chase,
Mirage of our souls, gentle grace.

Hidden truths and dreams untold,
Stories in the winds unfold.
Dancing flames of spirits bold,
Mirage of our souls, purest gold.

Reflection in Time

In a mirror, the past remains,
Lingered shadows of joy and pains.
Moments fleeting, like gentle rains,
Reflection in time, subtle chains.

Hours pass in the silence deep,
Memories awake from their sleep.
Emotions surface, soft and steep,
Reflection in time, secrets keep.

In the echoes of laughter's flight,
Glimpses of days, dark and bright.
Whispering tales in the night,
Reflection in time, endless sight.

As years cascade in their prime,
Melodies fade, then brightly chime.
Life's vast journey, a pantomime,
Reflection in time, pure sublime.

Echoes of Sentiment

Whispers of past in the wind's own song,
Luminescent dreams where old hopes belong,
Rekindling moments in twilight's embrace,
Hearts beat softly in memory's space.

Melancholy drips from the autumn leaves,
Through forgotten paths the spirit weaves,
Echoes deepen in the moon's pale light,
Sentiments linger in the quiet night.

Shadows converse on the river's edge,
Wishful thoughts form an unseen pledge,
Timeless stardust paints the evening sky,
Love's tender echo shall never die.

In the hush of dawn where secrets rest,
Soulful whispers make the heart confess,
Memories etched, forever to stay,
In the recess of mind, they softly play.

Expressions of Infinity

In the endless stretch of cosmic seas,
Where galaxies swirl like autumn leaves,
Stardust murmurs ancient lullabies,
Time and space blend in timeless eyes.

Infinity's dance in a star-kissed night,
Eternal verses in the soft twilight,
Planets converse in celestial tone,
Dreams of the vast, unknown and lone.

Celestial beings paint the skies so rare,
Infinite symbols twinkle with flair,
Mysteries wrapped in the night's embrace,
An endless journey through cosmic grace.

In the deep expanse where time dissolves,
Every soul and star together evolves,
Boundless whispers in the quiet void,
Expressions of infinity, never destroyed.

Veiled Contours

Beneath the shroud of shadows cast,
Silent echoes of bygone past,
Shapes emerge in the twilight hue,
Contours whisper of truths they knew.

Mist veils the secrets of the night,
Softly cloaked in the pale moonlight,
Forms take shape in the gentle dusk,
Mysteries hidden in nature's husk.

Figures unknown, in silhouette dance,
Guarded glances in a fleeting trance,
Whispers float on the evening air,
Veiled truths we barely dare.

Hints of stories in the night concealed,
Dreams and visions softly revealed,
Contours painted on a shadow's edge,
Secrets held in a solemn pledge.

Unrevealed Blessings

In the silent whispers of the morn,
Threads of fate in fabric worn,
Blessings hidden in each tender tear,
Unrevealed gifts in moments near.

Mystic paths where secrets tread,
Every dawn by quietude led,
Miracles wrapped in a hush so slight,
Unseen treasures spark the night.

In the heart's core where prayers reside,
Unrevealed truths they gently guide,
Hope's shimmer in the smallest things,
Life's soft music that nature sings.

Blessings cloaked in the day's soft beams,
Dreams encased in moonlit streams,
Unveiled slowly, by grace's design,
Life's hidden blessings, forever shine.

Essence of Being

In the quiet dawn, where dreams take flight,
A whisper soft as morning light.
Through shadows cast, and fears unweave,
We find the essence, hearts believe.

With every step on life's vast stage,
Though weary hands may turn the page.
In moments still, where time suspends,
The essence of being transcends.

Beneath the stars, where worlds align,
In fragments small, the grand design.
A cosmic dance, an ancient weave,
Our place within, we dare perceive.

Through joy and pain, the fleeting breath,
A cycle bound by life and death.
Yet in between, the soul's soft gleam,
Lies the essence, the endless dream.

Echoes of Our Hearts

In the stillness of the night,
Where the world turns out the light.
Echoes of our hearts arise,
Whispered truths, love's sweet reprise.

Through the chaos of the day,
In the words we fail to say.
Silent signals, eyes that meet,
Echoes of our hearts discreet.

Every touch and every sigh,
In moments passing, time slips by.
Yet the echoes linger on,
In the heart, where love is drawn.

Across the years, through distant lands,
Bound by fate's unseen hands.
In the silence, in the dark,
Echoes of our hearts embark.

Otherworldly Perception

In the spaces 'tween the stars,
Where the cosmos leaves its scars.
Otherworldly sights unfold,
Mysteries in silence told.

Through the veils of time and space,
Glimpses of a distant place.
In the whispers of the night,
Otherworldly truths ignite.

Beyond the realms of seen and known,
Lies a world of thought unshown.
Perceptions shift, horizons bend,
In the vastness without end.

Ancient songs of planets sing,
To the pulse of cosmic string.
Otherworldly visions share,
Secrets of the universe laid bare.

Traces in the Wind

In the dance of fleeting leaves,
Where the autumn wind deceives.
Traces of the past unwind,
Memories in the twilights bind.

Every gust, a phantom's touch,
In the whispers, saying much.
Echoes of the voices gone,
Traces in the wind live on.

Through the fields and through the trees,
In the sighs of gentle breeze.
Names and places once were dear,
Carried far yet always near.

Softly calls the wind's lament,
For the times in shadows spent.
In each breath, a life entwined,
In the wind, our traces find.

Echo of Our Souls

In silent nights, where whispers weave,
Our hearts align, where shadows cleave.
An echo heard from distant shores,
Resonates within, and much explores.

The moonlight dances on sacred grounds,
While secret songs in silence sound.
With every beat, our cadence grows,
An endless bond, that no one knows.

Through time and space, our spirits fly,
Beneath the stars, beneath the sky.
In dreams we meet, in timeless frames,
An echo of our silent claims.

Through whispered words, our vows remain,
A silent link that feels no strain.
Enduring love, that time consoles,
Forevermore, in the echo of our souls.

Whispered Dreams

In moonlit nights where shadows lay,
The stars align and light our way.
A secret world where dreams take flight,
In whispered tones, we meet each night.

Through velvet skies and silver streams,
We chase the light of endless dreams.
In quiet corners, hearts confess,
In whispered dreams, our souls undress.

The dawn no longer feels the same,
For in our dreams, we chased the flame.
Awake, but still within the gleam,
Of whispered hopes, our endless theme.

In twilight's glow, our wishes tied,
With whispered faith, we never hide.
For in the silence, we redeem,
Our love's pure truth, in whispered dreams.

Echoes of Our Connection

Through spaces vast and moments brief,
Our hearts connect beyond belief.
An echo felt with every beat,
Within, we find a love replete.

In twilight's grace, our spirits blend,
An unbroken line that will not end.
Across the void, with whispers sent,
In echoes true, our love's extent.

Where shadows dance and time retreats,
We find the place our souls complete.
An unseen cord that keeps us bound,
In echoes of the love we've found.

The sun may rise, the moon may wane,
But echoes of our love remain.
Through all the days in silent reflection,
We hear the echoes of our connection.

The Shape of Us

In sculpted dreams where shadows play,
We mold our hearts in night's ballet.
Each curve, each line, with gentle care,
Forms the shape of love we share.

Through whispered breath, our forms entwine,
In timeless dance, your hand in mine.
With every touch, our spirits fuse,
In shapes of love, we cannot lose.

Carved from whispers, drawn by light,
Our love takes form in softest night.
A masterpiece where souls collide,
In shapes of us, where love resides.

When dawn arrives and shadows fade,
The shape of us will not degrade.
Eternal forms in love's sculpted trust,
Forevermore, the shape of us.

Dreams of Us

In twilight's gentle whispered air,
Our dreams ignite without a care.
Hand in hand, we chase the stars,
Casting shadows near and far.

Echoes of laughter paint the sky,
Beneath the moon, just you and I.
Each heartbeat sings a love's refrain,
In dreams of us, we break the chain.

Fields of memories, lush and green,
We weave a world that's yet unseen.
With every kiss, the night unfolds,
A tapestry of love untold.

In slumber's arms, we'll find our place,
A universe in soft embrace.
Dreams of us, where time suspends,
Forever lovers, always friends.

Tomorrow's dawn, we'll bid goodbye,
But in our dreams, we'll always fly.
Through night and day, our spirits soar,
In dreams of us, we'll dream some more.

Illusions of Togetherness

We walk a path of mirrored light,
Togetherness in fleeting sight.
Reflections dance, a phantom's play,
In illusions, we find our way.

Whispers of what might have been,
Glances stolen, fleeting sin.
In shadows cast, we intertwine,
A love that's neither yours nor mine.

Fingers trace the lines of fate,
Timeless moments we create.
In dreams, we're whole and holding tight,
Illusions shimmer in the night.

Promises in whispered air,
A touch that fades, we disappear.
Yet in the heart, that phantom glow,
Illusions of togetherness grow.

A love unreal, a fleeting mist,
In shadows, shadows, we exist.
With every dawn, reality churns,
But in the heart, illusion burns.

Shadows of You

In the corners, shadows hide,
Echoes of you by my side.
Each silhouette, a memory,
A fragment of our history.

The night's embrace, your gentle touch,
In shadows, I miss you so much.
Your laughter lingers in the air,
A shadow's whisper, everywhere.

Moonlight casts its silver hue,
Upon the world, the shadowed you.
We dance beneath the starry night,
In shadows, holding on so tight.

A fleeting glimpse, a wisp of hair,
In shadows' grasp, I feel you there.
Your presence haunts the midnight hour,
Shadows of you, a ghostly flower.

When morning breaks, the shadows flee,
Yet in my heart, you'll always be.
In every dusk, your form takes view,
An endless dance, the shadows of you.

Fragments of Presence

Moments splinter like the dawn,
In fragments, presence carries on.
Each shard a piece of time we hold,
In hearts, their stories yet untold.

A smile, a look, a tender word,
In fragments, presence always heard.
Eternal echoes, we collect,
In fragments found, we reconnect.

Glimpses past and future blend,
Time's tapestry will never end.
In every seam, your thread is spun,
Fragments gleam, who we've become.

Though distance sets our paths apart,
In fragments, presence fills the heart.
Memories woven, tightly bound,
In fragments, you're forever found.

So when the world grows dark and cold,
In fragments, presence we behold.
Each piece a beacon, guiding true,
Forever fragments, always you.

Transparent Threads

In the loom of fate, we weave,
Threads unseen, lines interleave.
Gossamer moments, softly blend,
Tapestries time shall not rend.

Silver strands through shadows cast,
Binding futures, linking past.
Webs of hope and dreams profound,
In each silken thread, we're found.

Veins of light and hearts entwined,
Interlaced in space and mind.
Fragile bonds, yet strong, persist,
In this ancient, whispered mist.

Dew-kissed mornings break the day,
Unseen ties we lightly sway.
Symphonies of life unfold,
In these threads, our tales are told.

Softly woven, love and grace,
Transparent threads, a warm embrace.
Through each stitch, a story spun,
Together, till the world is one.

In the Mind's Eye

Imagine worlds where shadows dance,
In the silent realms of trance.
Visions flicker, softly bloom,
In the mind's eye, weave their loom.

Dreams that shimmer, whisper low,
Where the hidden waters flow.
Thoughts like stars ignite the night,
Lighting pathways out of sight.

Mirrored halls of memories,
Echoing like autumn's breeze.
Fleeting glimpses, faint and rare,
In the crevices of air.

Silent whispers, realms unseen,
In the spaces in-between.
Mystic tapestries, they fly,
In the mind's eye, reaching sky.

Endless vistas, boundless seas,
In the solitude and ease.
Visions that forever lie,
In the tender mind's own eye.

Echoes of Our Time

Eternal whispers through the night,
Echoes of our shared delight.
Moments fleeting, carved in rhyme,
In the silent dance of time.

Ancient stories, voices old,
Through the echoes, tales unfold.
Timeless songs of joy and pain,
Resonating once again.

Seasons change, yet linger still,
In the echoes, hearts fulfill.
Every laugh and every tear,
Ripples through the atmosphere.

Memories, a gentle breeze,
Through the endless forest trees.
Echoes of our past, we find,
Ever etched within the mind.

Time will pass, yet still remain,
In the echoes, all we gain.
Threads of history, intertwined,
Leading us, refined, aligned.

Whispered Essence

Softly spoken, like a dream,
Whispers flow in silent stream.
Hidden voices, truths confess,
In the night's soft, sweet caress.

In the moonlight's gentle beam,
Weaving through the heart's own seam.
Essence pure, in whispers found,
In the quiet, love unbound.

Breath of dawn, the world awakes,
Whispers rise as daybreak takes.
Sunlit tones on morning's crest,
In each whisper, find our rest.

Nature's song, a whispered plea,
In each leaf and swaying tree.
Essence of the earth and sky,
In soft whispers, they do sigh.

Faintly told, yet deeply heard,
In each heart, a whispered word.
Essence binds us, soul to soul,
Whispered secrets make us whole.

Celestial Connection

Beneath the stars, our souls unite,
A dance eternal, through the night.
In cosmic whispers, secrets shared,
A boundless love, beyond declared.

Through galaxies, our hearts do soar,
In universe, forever more.
A symphony of planets sing,
To loves' celestial, golden ring.

Among the nebulas we weave,
A tapestry, we'll not deceive.
Stars align, our fates entwined,
In night sky's canvas, paths defined.

Eclipsing moons, with shadows cast,
We find a love that holds so fast.
In stellar winds, our dreams align,
On astral currents, hearts entwine.

In cosmic dance, we find our peace,
In starlit realms, our spirits cease.
Infinity, our love shall hold,
In universe, our story told.

Vanishing Thoughts

In twilight hours, my thoughts do fade,
To realms where shadows cast their shade.
Ephemeral as the morning dew,
In vapor trails, my mind renew.

Elusive dreams, they swiftly pass,
Like fleeting footprints in the grass.
A whisper through the emerald leaves,
A truth that's hidden, time deceives.

Silent echoes from the past,
Memories, they never last.
A gentle touch, a fleeting glance,
Moments lost in dreamlike trance.

Phantoms of the mind retreat,
In shadows dark, they find their seat.
Yet in my heart, they softly gleam,
Vanishing thoughts, a silent dream.

As night descends, they fade away,
These thoughts that cannot bring the day.
In quiet stillness, calm remains,
Vanishing thoughts, elusive strains.

Glowing Embers

In hearth's embrace, the embers bright,
A warm and flickering, golden light.
The whispers of the flame do tell,
A story old, a timeless spell.

In shadows cast upon the wall,
The dance of fire, we heed its call.
A moment's pause, a gentle glow,
In burning warmth, our spirits grow.

The embers' tale of yesteryear,
In crackling whispers, we can hear.
A saga of the fireside lore,
Of love and loss, and days of yore.

As nights grows deep, the flames subdue,
Yet still, their warmth remains in view.
In glowing embers, hearts ignite,
Through fading fire, we find our light.

In glowing depths, our dreams abide,
In flickered hope, our fears we hide.
Eternal flame, a guiding star,
The glowing embers, near and far.

Clouded Sentiments

In misty haze, our thoughts align,
Within the clouds, emotions pine.
A veil of grey, our hearts envelop,
In quiet shroud, our feelings develop.

Shadows drift in skies above,
Reflecting hearts encased in love.
Through fog-filled air, we find our way,
In clouded sentiments, we sway.

Ephemeral as the morning mist,
Our hopes and dreams, the skies have kissed.
In vapor trails, our vows unfold,
Among the clouds, our stories told.

A gentle rain, a touch so light,
Cleansing hearts through day and night.
In clouded realms, we find our peace,
In billowed whispers, dreams release.

Ascend with me, to skies so high,
Where clouded sentiments confide.
In this ethereal, boundless sphere,
Our love, eternal, crystal clear.

Beyond the Visible

Through veils of mist, the valleys sleep,
Beneath the star-kissed sky so deep.
An endless quest in shadows' keep,
To places where our dreams then leap.

Whispers hum through ancient trees,
Abiding truths on twilight's breeze.
In shadows cast by moonlit seas,
We find the secrets none can seize.

Mysteries hidden in the dawn,
Reveal the worlds our eyes look on.
A fleeting glimpse, then they are gone,
To realms where silent hopes are drawn.

The horizon calls with tones unknown,
An echo of our souls' long moan.
In whispered verse, our seeds are sown,
In gardens where the stars are grown.

The fabric of the night reveals,
A myriad of cosmic seals.
In quiet realms where silence heals,
We walk beyond what sight conceals.

Shared Glimmers

A moment caught in golden light,
A glance that turns the weary bright.
Shared glimmers in the depth of night,
Two souls converge, a single flight.

Through laughter's sound and silent tear,
In every joy and whispered fear.
We find the ties that draw us near,
In bonds of love that persevere.

In starlit skies and morning dew,
A promise shared by hearts so true.
In every shade, in every hue,
A timeless tale begins anew.

When shadows fall and days grow dim,
Together, we a thread will spin.
Through every trial, though hopes be thin,
Our light remains, a glow within.

We walk the path, both bound and free,
In rhythm, like the vast blue sea.
For in each shared eternity,
We find the grace of you and me.

Enchanted Reveries

In dreams where realms of wonder lie,
Where stardust paints the midnight sky.
An echo of the heart's soft sigh,
In enchanted reveries we fly.

The silver rivers softly gleam,
In lands adorned by twilight's beam.
Our spirits sail on every stream,
Boundless in our soulful dream.

In gardens where the moonlight plays,
And whispers weave through twilight's haze.
We wander through those mystic days,
Lost in the glow of astral rays.

A dance as ancient as the stars,
Through time and space, no wound or scars.
In reveries where there's no bars,
We find the truth of who we are.

In realms unseen by waking eyes,
Lie hidden realms beyond the skies.
Our souls await the grand surprise,
In enchanted reveries, we rise.

Infinite Bounds

In fields where time and space converge,
Where stars and dreams in dance merge.
A place where endless echoes surge,
Beyond the finite's gentle dirge.

To journey forth with open mind,
In lands where limits none can bind.
Infinite bounds in realms we find,
Where heart and cosmos are aligned.

In every grain of sand and stone,
The whispers of the infinite are sown.
A universe within each tone,
In silent symphonies unknown.

Through galaxies in silent flight,
We journey forth on beams of light.
To places where day meets the night,
In endless bounds of pure delight.

Forevermore we drift and soar,
In endless bounds of cosmic lore.
Our spirits free, our spirits explore,
The infinite—a boundless shore.

Gossamer Bonds

In threads of light, our spirits met,
Through whispers soft and rare.
A dance of souls, a silver net,
With love beyond compare.

In veils of dusk, two shadows blend,
A weave of dreams so fond.
Through silent winds, our hearts extend,
In gossamer-like bond.

An echo's call through twilight's seam,
A tender touch divine.
Through trembling night, a fleeting gleam,
Your gaze returns to mine.

A lacing breath, a moment held,
Through fate's uncertain sway.
Our paths entwined, desire spelled,
In twilight's gentle play.

With every step, a promise sworn,
A tether softly drawn.
In gossamer bonds, our hearts adorn,
Until the break of dawn.

Glimpse of Eternity

In fleeting stars, a vision spark,
A glimpse of endless night.
Through shadows deep and canvased dark,
Eternity takes flight.

In rivers made of astral threads,
Time's secrets softly flow.
Our dreams aloft on feathered beds,
Where timeless whispers go.

Through ageless fields of silken space,
A dance of light and lore.
Infinity in soft embrace,
With echoes evermore.

In galaxies that silently twirl,
A silent testament.
A universe's whispered swirl,
Where heights and depths are blent.

In cosmic tapestries alight,
A truth sublime and free.
Through skies of ever-twinkling night,
A glimpse of eternity.

Subtle Existence

In silence found, a presence still,
A subtle, fleeting grace.
Through quiet dawns, the heart's refill,
In whispers soft, efface.

A gentle breeze, a tender sign,
Life's essence lightly born.
Through morning's light, in silver line,
Existence softly worn.

On paths where shadows gently blend,
A trace of being shown.
In realms where silent truths transcend,
Existence lightly sown.

With every breath, a world unseen,
A realm of secret might.
Through veils of dreams in emerald sheen,
Life's subtle touch alight.

In fleeting moments, time dispels,
A world of muted glow.
Through subtle signs and winding spells,
Existence softly flows.

Faint Impressions

On parchment skies, a hint of light,
In dawn's first whispered sigh.
Through tender hues, a fading night,
Beneath the soft-hued sky.

In shadows cast by morning's breath,
A trace of dreams now gone.
A meeting place of life and death,
Where memories are drawn.

A petal's fall, a feather's drift,
In air with stardust strewn.
Through gentle touch, our spirits lift,
In faint impressions hewn.

Through fleeting glimpses, time will tell,
Of moments brushed by fate.
In echoes soft, a silent spell,
In twilight's shifting gate.

Within the heart, a whisper's trace,
Of love's enduring song.
In faint impressions, life finds grace,
A place where souls belong.

Hints of You

In twilight's gentle glow, I'd stand,
Recalling whispers in the sand.
Your laughter like a cooling breeze,
Brings a memory that never leaves.

Starlit skies hold secrets near,
In every silent, falling tear.
Dew-kissed mornings, soft and true,
Hold timeless hints of you.

Melodies we once composed,
In heart's recesses, forever enclosed.
Thoughts of you in night's embrace,
Wander in this quiet space.

Amidst the dawn's first morning light,
Lies an echo of our flight.
In every shadow, every hue,
I find the hints of you.

Through life's shifting, endless dance,
I hold onto our love's expanse.
Though years may pass and seasons change,
The hints of you remain.

Unrevealed Essence

Veiled within the morning's dew,
An essence quiet, pure, and true.
In shadows cast by fleeting night,
Lies a secret, hidden tight.

Mysteries whisper on the breeze,
A silent song among the trees.
In eyes that glance but do not see,
Dwells a truth not meant for me.

Underneath the surface calm,
Echoes of an unheard psalm.
Fragments of a story old,
An essence waiting to unfold.

In the hush of twilight's beam,
Drifts a half-remembered dream.
Through the veil of night's serene,
Hides an essence yet unseen.

In thoughts unspoken, words unsaid,
Lie the paths we haven't tread.
In every heart's unseen recess,
Lingers the unrevealed essence.

Silent Musings

Gentle whispers in the night,
Silent musings, pure delight.
Thoughts that wander through the air,
Floating in the quiet there.

Stars that shimmer, soft and bright,
Echo secrets in their light.
Silent musings, softly tread,
In the space between what's said.

Dreams that wander far and wide,
In the stillness, side by side.
Silent musings, tenderly,
Paint a world we cannot see.

Through the hours of darkest hue,
Silent musings, born anew.
In the calm, a harmony,
Silent whispers, wild and free.

Heartfelt dreams without a sound,
In the silence, truth is found.
Silent musings, ever near,
Speak the words we long to hear.

Fleeting Embrace

In moments brief, our paths entwine,
A fleeting touch, a whisper fine.
In the space of heartbeat's grace,
We shared a fleeting embrace.

Time stands still as gazes meet,
In the dance of life, bittersweet.
In those seconds, pure and clear,
You were close, and I was near.

Moments pass, like grains of sand,
Slip through fingers, lost and grand.
Yet in memories' gentle trace,
Lingers our fleeting embrace.

Days may blur and seasons change,
Still, that touch feels not so strange.
In the corners of my mind,
A fleeting embrace I find.

Though the world keeps spinning fast,
Holding tightly to the past,
In each quiet, tender place,
Lives our fleeting embrace.

Boundless Moments

In a symphony of endless skies,
Where dreams and moments intertwine,
Each whisper that the wind supplies,
Carries a love that's purely thine.

Time dances with a gleeful grace,
Unfettered by the world's confines,
As stars align in boundless space,
Our spirits free, our hearts align.

Eclipsed beneath the midnight hues,
We find our solace in the night,
With every breath, a page to use,
For crafting tales of pure delight.

The morning dew on petals bright,
Reflects the dawn of newfound day,
In boundless moments, pure and light,
We navigate life's vast ballet.

So let us cherish, hold and keep,
These fleeting seconds, hours cast,
For in our hearts, they'll always sleep,
In boundless moments, made to last.

Traces in Time

There's an echo in the ancient breeze,
Of stories written long before,
Here lies the secrets, memories,
Of lives we've lived and long adored.

The footprints left on paths we trod,
Impressions time will never fade,
Within the earth, beneath the sod,
Lie whispers of the marks we've made.

In fleeting days and nights so brief,
We carve our names into the clay,
As sand and tide steal time like a thief,
Yet traces of us still will stay.

The moments past, the days ahead,
Are threads within the grand design,
Though our bodies one day shed,
We'll remain in traces, intertwined.

So cherish time, each fleeting hour,
In every act, in every rhyme,
We live in love, we live in power,
Eternal traces in the sands of time.

Silent Affection

In quiet glances, hearts entwine,
A love that words can scarce convey,
With every beat, with every sign,
In silence, love has found its way.

Beneath the moon's soft silver glow,
Our souls connect without a sound,
In tranquil moments, whispers flow,
In silent affection, love is found.

The touch of hands, the gentle gaze,
Speaks louder than the loudest cheer,
In stillness of the world's malaise,
Our silent love, so pure and clear.

No need for words, no voice to raise,
In every breath, in every sight,
God's gift, our everlasting praise,
In silence, love burns ever bright.

So let us walk the silent night,
With hearts aligned in true perfection,
For in our quiet, we find light,
And live within our silent affection.

Glimpses of Eternity

Amidst the stars, in endless night,
We find the glimpse of what could be,
A universe bathed in soft light,
Revealing glimpses of eternity.

The cycles of the moon and sun,
A dance as old as time began,
In every dawn, a life begun,
In every dusk, eternal plan.

The seasons change, the rivers flow,
Mountains rise and seas expand,
Through all, the seeds of love we sow,
We glimpse eternity in our hand.

In moments shared and dreams we chase,
A timeless truth in fleeting hands,
The infinite within the space,
Of every breath that life commands.

So in this life, both wild and free,
Let's cherish every memory,
For in our hearts, we'll always see,
The fleeting glimpses of eternity.

Woven Dreams

Threads of twilight softly whisper
In the loom of night's caress,
Where the fabric of our wishes
Forms a tapestry of rest.

Stars are beads that gently shimmer,
Patterns stitched by moonlight's gleam,
In this quilt of quiet wonder,
We are cradled by our dreams.

Softly woven aspirations,
Intertwine with hopes unseen,
Binding close our deepest longings,
Crafted from night's silken sheen.

Nebulous and ever shifting,
Morphing shapes in shadow's grasp,
Woven dreams in night assembling,
In their tender hold, we clasp.

Fragmented Stardust

Cosmic whispers drift on ether,
Echoes from the vast unknown,
Fragmented shards of ancient stardust,
Falling soft like twilight's stone.

Galaxies in jeweled splendor,
Scatter light like teardrop spray,
Through the void, a trail of memories,
Guiding lost souls on their way.

Timeless voices in the silence,
Speak in tongues of nebulae,
We are fragments of the cosmos,
Fleeting sparks of endless sky.

In the night, we see our essence,
Mirror shards of what could be,
Fragmented stardust, dreams unspoken,
Drifting back to infinity.

Soul's Reflection

In the quiet ponds of twilight,
Ripples spread from thoughts unseen,
Soul's reflection softly shimmering,
On the surface, still and keen.

Glimpses of our hidden wonders,
Dance upon the mirrored lake,
As the moonlight casts its magic,
And the dreams within us wake.

Shadows of our deepest longings,
With the night begin to play,
Revealing truths in gentle whispers,
That the sunlight hides away.

In these waters clear and tender,
See the depths of our intent,
Soul's reflection, pure and endless,
In the night's embrace is spent.

Subtle Symphony

Notes of night in subtle symphony,
Softly hum the world to sleep,
Crickets join the moonlit chorus,
In the darkness, secrets keep.

Whispers of the breeze in concert,
Rustling leaves and swaying trees,
Nature's lullaby unfolding,
Filling hearts with peaceful ease.

Stars above twinkling in rhythm,
Cosmic harmony on high,
Guiding dreams on silver pathways,
Through the canvas of the sky.

Each serene nocturnal measure,
Plays a tune both sweet and grand,
Subtle symphony of silence,
Weaves its magic through the land.

Portraits of Presence

In moments soft, the world stands still,
Time's tender hand does linger,
A canvas painted with silent quill,
Imprinted by life's finger.

Each breath a brushstroke, pure and light,
Emotions cast in hues,
A dance of shadows, day to night,
In nature's timeless muse.

From dawn to dusk, the scenes unfold,
A gallery so vast,
The stories whispered, gently told,
In echoes of the past.

In faces etched by fleeting years,
Reside the tales unspoken,
A mosaic formed of joys and tears,
In every heart a token.

So cherish now, the fleeting glance,
The presence, deeply felt,
For in life's brief and hurried dance,
Our very souls are knelt.

Beyond the Horizon

Where the sky and earth embrace,
In a kiss of endless blue,
Lies a realm of boundless space,
A world both old and new.

The silent call of distant shores,
Whispers of the unknown,
A promise born of ancient lore,
Where the seeds of dreams are sown.

With every step, a venture bold,
Past twilight's fading light,
Through mists of gold, the future's fold,
Unveiled by morning's sight.

Mountains tall and valleys deep,
Guard secrets yet untold,
In shadows cast, the echoes keep,
The mystery they hold.

So sail beyond the horizon's edge,
Where dreams and stars collide,
For life is but a fleeting pledge,
In the vast, eternal tide.

Ephemeral Glances

A glimmer in the passing light,
A sparkle in the dawn,
Moments fleeting, pure and bright,
Before they too are gone.

Each glance a page from time's own book,
Written in the air,
A stolen second, just to look,
At beauty, brief and rare.

The autumn leaf, its journey brief,
Dances in the breeze,
A sigh of life, both sweet and grief,
Whispered through the trees.

In ripples on a moonlit lake,
The fleeting images form,
A mirror of the life we make,
In every breath we warm.

So seize each moment, hold it close,
In memory's soft lance,
For life itself, as we all know,
Is but an ephemeral glance.

Mysteries Unveiled

Beneath the veil of night, so deep,
Lie secrets dark and wide,
In shadows where the quiet sleep,
Life's mysteries reside.

The stars that dot the inky sky,
A map of ancient tales,
Through cosmic whispers, low and high,
The universe unveils.

In whispered winds of twilight's breath,
In echoes of the past,
The dance of life, the song of death,
Both slow and wondrous, vast.

The endless quest for truths unfound,
Through forests dense and wild,
In every heart, a silent sound,
The ache of knowing, mild.

So venture forth, with eyes alight,
Through realms both dark and veiled,
For in the endless quest for light,
Our deepest truths are hailed.

Interwoven Souls

Upon the threads of fate, we dance,
Two spirits in a timeless trance.
Bound by bonds unseen, we glide,
Interwoven, side by side.

In shadows dark and dawn's soft hue,
Our echoes sing, as whispers do.
No distance vast, nor time's cruel toll,
Can part the weave of soul from soul.

With every breath, a silent vow,
With every heartbeat, here and now.
A tapestry of dreams we weave,
In endless love, we both believe.

Knit by hands of cosmic grace,
In every life, in every place.
Fingers entwined, hearts unfold,
As one, together, growing old.

In the starlight's gentle gleam,
In every tear, in every dream.
Our souls are threads, both tight and free,
A union that shall ever be.

Beyond the Facade

Behind each smile, a hidden story lies,
A world unseen, beneath our skies.
Eyes that sparkle, hold deep pain,
A mask we wear, in sun and rain.

Layers thick, we build our walls,
Guarding whispers, silent calls.
Yet through the cracks, light may seep,
Revealing truths, we dare to keep.

In mirrored glass, reflections dance,
A fleeting glance, a second chance.
To see beyond, the painted face,
To touch the heart, with gentle grace.

Through myriad lines, etched by time,
Lies a soul, seeking to find.
Connections pure, beyond the show,
Real and raw, where spirits flow.

In every heart, a world confined,
A universe, both bold and kind.
Beyond the facade, we truly see,
The boundless depths of you and me.

Fragments of Light

Scattered beams, in twilight's veil,
Whispers of light, through shadows sail.
Moments brief, yet burning bright,
Fragments of an endless night.

In every shard, a story told,
Glimmers of hopes, both new and old.
A cosmic dance, of dark and light,
In balance held, through endless flight.

Pieces small, of dreams we chase,
In every dawn, another trace.
Of joy and pain, a mingled hue,
A palette of our lives in view.

Through prisms of our inner sight,
We catch the sparks, the pure delight.
Of fleeting time, in captured rays,
Fractal tapestries amaze.

In every fragment, lives a whole,
A mirrored depth, of soul to soul.
Bright and bold, or soft and slight,
Together form, our human light.

Heartfelt Enigmas

In chambers deep, where secrets lie,
Our hearts conceal, and yet, they try.
To speak in tongues, of love's own rhyme,
Unraveling enigmas, bound by time.

Through silent sighs, and laughter sweet,
Encounters brief, where worlds do meet.
Our souls converse, in whispers light,
Heartfelt enigmas, endless night.

In cryptic notes, of feelings blurred,
In unspoken words, often heard.
A touch, a glance, a knowing too,
Encodes the bond, twixt me and you.

With every beat, a puzzle piece,
A mystery that will not cease.
To weave its tale of hidden lore,
Of love and life's forevermore.

Within the heart, a riddle stays,
As timeless as the passing days.
Heartfelt enigmas, deep and true,
A silent song, 'tween me and you.

Ghostly Glimpses

In the shadows of the night,
phantoms waltz with fading light.
Whispers dance upon the breeze,
silent echoes through the trees.

Footsteps fall on cold, damp ground,
distant moans, a haunting sound.
Flickers of forgotten days,
along these ghostly, winding ways.

Memories lost, yet found anew,
in spectral shades of twilight's hue.
A bridge between the realms of past,
where spirits tread and shadows cast.

In the mirror's winking glass,
the ghostly glimpses briefly pass.
Eyes of sorrow, hearts of flame,
calling softly, name by name.

Come the dawn, they fade away,
as night surrenders to the day.
Yet in the depth of darkened hours,
they hold their silent, haunting powers.

Shifting Echoes

In a canyon deep and wide,
voices travel far and hide.
Bound by time, yet free to drift,
in a dance of echoes swift.

Softly calling, then they fade,
whispers in the night's cascade.
Tales of old and secrets new,
shifting echoes, passing through.

Ripples in the air they leave,
traces none can quite perceive.
Unseen forces, strong and free,
weaving through eternity.

In the heart, they resonate,
mystic tunes they generate.
Songs that none can truly hear,
yet to souls, they still endear.

Shifting echoes, timeless find,
threads that intertwine and bind.
In their wake, the world awakes,
with each sound the silence breaks.

Mirage of Love

In the desert's vast embrace,
mirages dance with fleeting grace.
Love appears on shifting sands,
a touch that slips through eager hands.

Eyes behold a distant gleam,
in the heart, a tender dream.
Yet like vapor, it recedes,
in its place, a longing breeds.

Tides of passion, waves of fire,
sparkle with a bright desire.
But as the sun sets in the west,
illusions lay the heart to rest.

Yearned for in a fleeting glance,
promised only in a trance.
A kiss of wind, a whispered sigh,
leaving questions, asking why.

Still we chase this phantom light,
in the hopes of love's delight.
Through the sands of time we rove,
seeking the mirage of love.

Omnipresent Whispers

Through the skies of endless blue,
whispers carry, swift and true.
In the winds, a voice is heard,
echoing without a word.

In the rustle of the leaves,
in the sigh of ocean's eaves.
Secrets spoken, subtle, clear,
whispers that are always near.

In the hush of twilight's glow,
softly singing, whispers flow.
Thoughts and dreams alight the air,
sharing stories everywhere.

In the night, when all is still,
whispers flutter, climb, and thrill.
From the stars, they drift below,
tales they only wish to show.

Omnipresent, ever part,
these whispers bind both heart to heart.
As we listen, they confide,
in their gentle, quiet tide.

Radiant Mirage

In the desert's golden embrace,
Mirages dance, elusive grace,
Sunlight glitters, sandbells chime,
Whispers of an endless time.

Rippling air, a fleeting sight,
Dreams dissolve in blinding light,
Oasis beckons, just ahead,
Illusions drift, like words unsaid.

Mirrored sky in amber waves,
Secreting truths the desert craves,
Mysteries in every grain,
Whispers soft as summer rain.

Journey endless, steps untold,
Chasing glimmers made of gold,
Ephemeral as dawn's first blush,
Radiant mirage, a timeless hush.

Infinite horizon's call,
Where shadows rise, then gently fall,
Wandering through realms unknown,
Seeking dreams out on our own.

Lingering Echoes

Mountains cold, and valleys deep,
Where memories in silence keep,
Footprints left in time's soft snow,
Lingering echoes, whispers low.

Every whisper tells a tale,
Lives entwined in fate's cruel gale,
Voices past, and futures bright,
Merging in the quiet night.

Hollow wind through ancient trees,
Murming secrets with the breeze,
Past and present intertwine,
Echoes in a realm divine.

Time's embrace, a ghostly hand,
Leveraging a world unplanned,
Every breath a fleeting sound,
Echoes in the soul profound.

In the stillness, hearts align,
Through the corridors of time,
Echoes linger, softly yearn,
Teaching us the way to turn.

Phantom Whispers

Midnight mists and shadows play,
Phantom whispers, night's ballet,
Secrets murmured, soft and clear,
Stealthy words that none can hear.

Curtains flutter, breath of night,
Whispers drift away from sight,
Ghostly murmurs, spectral sigh,
Echoes of a lullaby.

Haunted halls and moonlit beams,
Phantoms weave their silent dreams,
Hearts awaken, spellbound trance,
Caught within the night's advance.

Wintry wind with gentle grace,
Stirring whispers, soft embrace,
Voices lost in time's expanse,
Phantom whispers' secret dance.

In the hush where shadows meet,
Souls entwine in silence sweet,
Phantom whispers, tales unfold,
Mysteries of night retold.

Elusive Harmony

Between the notes of a gentle song,
Where cadence flows and dreams belong,
Elusive harmony we chase,
Fleeting whispers leave no trace.

In twilight's glow, a melody,
A haunting, distant symphony,
Through time's shadows, softly trails,
Harmony's enchanting veils.

Stars align in silent score,
Cosmic rhythms evermore,
Songs of spheres in vast expanse,
Harmony in timeless dance.

Selene's glow and solar gleam,
Weaving through an endless dream,
Seeking balance, perfect rhyme,
Harmony beyond our time.

Listen close, the heart's own plea,
Chasing dreams of unity,
In life's song, the soul's delight,
Elusive harmony, pure light.

Moments of Us

Beneath the twilight's gentle glow,
In whispers soft, our secrets flow,
We trace the stars in endless sky,
Together, where the dreams comply.

In fields of gold, where daisies bloom,
Our laughter dances, chases gloom,
The world around us fades to gray,
When in your eyes, I lose my way.

From morning dew to night's embrace,
A silent vow in time and space,
Hands entwined, a perfect fit,
In every glance, our spirits lit.

Through winding paths and ocean's roar,
Each step with you, I crave some more,
A journey etched in heart and mind,
In moments of us, love defined.

Silent Conversations

Between two hearts, a quiet beat,
In silent rooms, our spirits meet,
No words are spoken, yet so loud,
In shadows where our dreams are plowed.

Through looks and sighs, we speak in hues,
A language old, yet ever new,
Our minds in tandem, thoughts align,
In stillness, secrets so divine.

The ticking clock, a solemn friend,
Yet in its march, we find no end,
Encapsulated in the now,
We share ambitions, wordless vow.

In every silence, stories told,
In every breath, our bond is bold,
Unseen, unheard, yet deeply known,
In silent conversations, flown.

Unseen Connection

Invisible threads that bind our souls,
An unseen weave that love controls,
Through space and time, a whisper clear,
Connecting hearts, so close, so near.

Without a touch, yet deeply felt,
In shared dreams where our thoughts have dwelt,
A symphony of silent chords,
In this, our unseen love records.

Across the miles, no distance true,
Our spirits dance in skies so blue,
Bound not by sight, but by the heart,
United, though we're miles apart.

In echoes soft and shadows bright,
We find each other in the night,
An unseen bond, both pure and strong,
In this connection, we belong.

Phantom Presence

In phantom whispers, shadows play,
Your presence haunts the light of day,
A ghostly touch, a spectral kiss,
In every breath, your spirit's bliss.

I trace your steps in empty halls,
In mirrored glass, where silence calls,
Though not in sight, you're always near,
A phantom presence, ever clear.

Your essence lingers in the air,
A phantom's love beyond compare,
In dreams, you're real, in life, unseen,
Yet everywhere, and in between.

In hearts that ache, in minds that yearn,
Your phantom presence will return,
Untethered, yet forever bind,
In every thought, my love defined.

Unwritten Stories

Beneath the sky, where whispers play,
In fields where dreams and moments sway,
Unwritten stories hide away,
In silence, they await their day.

Each leaf that falls, a tale untold,
In whispers of the wind so cold,
They gather 'round the hearts so bold,
Awaiting words, a story's gold.

The stars at night, with secrets bright,
They shed a tear, a glistening light,
For every soul, a quiet right,
To tell the tales that drift from sight.

The rivers run with stories keen,
Through valleys lush and forests green,
They carve the paths where dreams have been,
In murmurs soft and sights unseen.

So pen the tales that long to be,
And set them free, a boundless sea,
For in each heart lives poetry,
The unwritten stories, our decree.

Beyond the Surface

A mirror's face, it hides the soul,
Where shadows dance and stories roll,
Beyond the surface, whispers stroll,
In depths of hearts, the truth consol.

The eyes that see may not perceive,
The love and loss that hearts believe,
For what we show and what we weave,
Are but reflections, make-believe.

The ocean's depth, a mystic haze,
It holds the quiet, hidden maze,
Beyond the surface, thoughts amaze,
In silent songs and dreamy gaze.

Beneath the mask, a world concealed,
With scars and smiles yet revealed,
The tender truths, softly healed,
In whispers, mysteries unsealed.

So look beyond what eyes may see,
And find the soul in subtle plea,
For in the depths of you and me,
Resides the heart, wild and free.

Veil of Dreams

Through mist and shadow, dreams reside,
In hidden realms where secrets hide,
The veil of dreams, a silent guide,
To realms where hopes and hearts collide.

In twilight's breath, the visions rise,
With wings of night and dawn's disguise,
They soar beyond the waking eyes,
In lands of starlit, soft surprise.

Beneath the moon's enchanting beams,
Lie woven worlds and midnight schemes,
The quiet hum of restless streams,
In whispers of the veil of dreams.

Each slumbered touch, a fleeting stay,
In gardens where the shadows play,
The veil of dreams, a night's ballet,
Where echoes of the heart convey.

So drift within the dreamer's lens,
Where fantasies and truths amends,
In veils of night, where longing bends,
Find the peace where dreaming ends.

Unseen Affections

In shadows where the whispers talk,
Unseen affections gently walk,
In quiet hearts, they leave their mark,
A tender light within the dark.

A silent glance, a hidden grace,
Affections bloom in secret space,
They flourish in a soft embrace,
Unseen, yet hold a tranquil trace.

In stolen moments, fleeting, rare,
With silent sighs that fill the air,
Unspoken words of love declare,
In quiet times, beyond compare.

The gentle brush of hands in flight,
Affections soar, a quiet might,
In unseen realms, they find their light,
A silent star within the night.

So cherish what the eyes can't find,
And listen close with heart aligned,
For unseen affections, pure and kind,
Are whispers of the soul combined.

Unseen Echoes

In the stillness, whispers loom,
Their gentle murmurs break the gloom.
Secrets dance in silent night,
Echoes hidden from our sight.

Faint as shadows on a wall,
Memories from ages call.
Through the veils of mist they weave,
Unseen echoes, hearts deceive.

Soft vibrations, unheard cries,
Resonate where silence lies.
Unspoken words float on the breeze,
Carried over tranquil seas.

In the quiet, we can hear,
Fleeting dreams that draw us near.
Ancient voices, once discerned,
Lost in echoes, never spurned.

From the past to future's gaze,
Subtle as a twilight haze.
Echoes linger, faint yet true,
Unseen, waiting to renew.

Shimmering Illusions

Glimmering lights, an endless dance,
Caught within a dreamlike trance.
Mirrors twist in moonlit streams,
Shimmering illusions, fragile seams.

Reflections sway upon the floor,
Waves of light in astral lore.
Shadows blend with fleeting glow,
Mysteries only night can know.

Through the smoke and ethereal haze,
Shapes emerge in dazzling blaze.
Chimeras born of light's embrace,
In this world, they find their place.

As dawn approaches, they fade to gray,
Ephemeral dreams begin to stray.
Yet in the glow of twilight's kiss,
Shimmering illusions still persist.

In every glint, a whispered tale,
Of dreams that in the darkness sail.
Epiphanies that hearts pursue,
Shimmering, shimmering, ever true.

Ethereal Bonds

Beneath the stars, where shadows meet,
Spirits in a dance so sweet.
Ties unseen by mortal eyes,
Ethereal bonds that never die.

Threads of light stretch far and wide,
Binding hearts from side to side.
Wisps of hope and love's refrain,
Eternal links that bear no chain.

Through the void, they come and go,
Tides that ebb and gently flow.
Invisible, yet deeply felt,
In every heart, these bonds have dwelt.

In a realm beyond the veil,
Where time and space seem thin and frail,
Souls connect in silent grace,
Ethereal bonds that life embrace.

As the night gives way to day,
These bonds of light will guide our way.
Unseen forces, strong and grand,
Ethereal bonds, hand in hand.

Veiled Affection

Behind the mask, emotions hide,
Feelings deep and undenied.
Veiled affection, whispers soft,
Love that soars in silence, oft.

Eyes that speak without a sound,
Hearts where secret dreams are found.
Gestures light as morning dew,
Veiled affection, brave and true.

In the glance, a hidden plea,
Words unspoken, wild and free.
In the shadows, tender care,
Veiled affection, always there.

A touch unnoticed, fleeting grace,
Moments caught in time's embrace.
Silent vows within the night,
Veiled affection, pure delight.

Though the veil is gossamer thin,
Love resides deep within.
In every glance, a secret song,
Veiled affection, ever strong.

Silent Serenades

In twilight's hush, where whispers fade,
The moonlight casts its secret shade.
Dreams unfold like silken threads,
In silent serenades, our hearts are led.

Stars sprinkle lullabies in night,
Guiding lost souls with gentle light.
Beneath the canopy of sky's embrace,
Wishes dance in a timeless space.

Echoes of longing in the breeze,
Melodies that put minds at ease.
Midnight calls in hushed refrains,
Silent serenades through hidden lanes.

The world in slumber's sweet repose,
Where every moment softly flows.
Hearts entwine in whispered sighs,
Underneath the starlit skies.

Serenades in silence, pure and true,
Where fantasy and dreams accrue.
In night's arms, where shadows play,
Silent serenades fade with the day.

Uncharted Tendencies

Through realms of wonder, paths untold,
We venture forth, the brave and bold.
Unknown horizons, vast and wide,
Uncharted tendencies, side by side.

Curiosity, a guiding star,
Leads us to places near and far.
Where dreams and fears in silence blend,
Adventures born around each bend.

In lands where maps have never shown,
We find the seeds of wonders sown.
New footsteps trace untamed expanse,
With every gaze, a furtive glance.

Our hearts, they whisper tales unseen,
Of distant hopes and might-have-beens.
Through twilight's haze, and morning gleam,
We chase the thrill of wildest dreams.

In corridors of time unframed,
Lives unfold, and none are tamed.
With spirits free and eyes that see,
Uncharted tendencies, endlessly.

A Soul's Impression

In the calm of dawn's first light,
Awakened hearts take gentle flight.
Echoes of dreams from night's embrace,
Leave a soul's impression on every face.

Moments swirl, like whispers deep,
In memory's vault, forever keep.
Sorrows, joys, and fleeting sights,
In tender strokes of life's delights.

Time etches lines, both dark and bright,
On fragile canvases of might.
Each heartbeat marks, with subtle grace,
A soul's impression, time can't erase.

Through trials met and paths unknown,
Resilience in our spirits grown.
Leaves behind a tale to tell,
Of whispered secrets, we know well.

In final breaths, our essence stays,
Held within those fleeting days.
Impressions deep, a silent flow,
A soul's imprint, a tender glow.

Secret Frequencies

Beneath the hum of city breath,
Lie secret frequencies, depth on depth.
Invisible streams of whispered sound,
In hidden currents, life is found.

Unseen waves, on pathways glide,
Connecting hearts both far and wide.
In silent symphony they play,
Secret frequencies, night and day.

Between the beats of silence heard,
Messages blend, without a word.
Mysteries in the ether dwell,
Tales untold, in pulses swell.

Listeners of the wise attune,
To hidden rhythms, hidden tunes.
With hearts attuned, they sense and feel,
Secret frequencies, quiet and real.

In the spaces between spoken line,
There rests a secret, pure and fine.
An unbroken stream, in every beat,
Secret frequencies, life's quiet feat.

Luminous Mirage

In the desert's endless sprawl,
Mirages dance, elusive, bright.
Shimmering visions rise and fall,
Vanishing in the blistering light.

A fleeting hope, a ghostly dream,
Glimpses of an untouched spring.
In the mirage, we find a theme,
Of shadows where our wishes cling.

Golden dunes beneath the sun,
Whispers of a secret shore.
Chasing phantoms one by one,
Yearning, searching evermore.

Oasis found in fleeting gleam,
An echo of what might have been.
Mirage dissolves like morning steam,
Leaving dust where dreams have seen.

In the heart of endless sands,
Wanderers trust their eyes no more.
Luminous mirage in distant lands,
Captures souls forevermore.

Resonance of Hearts

In the quiet, hearts resound,
Echoes soft, a silent song.
Love's sweet melody profound,
In each heartbeat, pure and strong.

Two souls find a common beat,
Rhythms blend in perfect time.
From their union, joy replete,
Harmony in love's sweet rhyme.

Through the trials, through the tears,
Hearts endure, their cadence true.
In the darkest nights and years,
Love's refrain, they misconstrue.

When apart, the echoes fade,
Dissonant and incomplete.
Yet in dreams, they'll serenade,
Bound by hearts that ever meet.

In the sacred silence shared,
Hearts align, forever chime.
Resonance of love declared,
Beats as one, a timeless rhyme.

Fragments of Whispered Promises

Beneath the moonlit, silent skies,
Whispers drift on twilight breeze.
Promises in gentle guise,
Secrets carried through the trees.

Lovers' vows in hushed tones spoken,
Pledges lost to time's swift flight.
Fragments of a heart once open,
Scatter on the winds of night.

Silent echoes of caressed dreams,
Shadows of what might have been.
In the night, a distant gleam,
Of whispered words we can't unpin.

Promises, like dew, disperse,
Evaporate with morning's ray.
Love's sweet whisper turns to verse,
Etched in hearts, till break of day.

Yet in dreams, those vows return,
Ghosts of whispers, soft and clear.
In fragments, tender hearts will yearn,
For promises they'd hold so dear.

In Between Beats

Moments lapse in silent grace,
In the spaces, stillness reigns.
Time suspended, love's embrace,
In between beats, life remains.

Breathless pauses, eyes connect,
Heartbeats echo, whisper low.
Words unspoken have effect,
In between the beats, they flow.

In the pauses, we find truth,
Silent glances speak aloud.
Love transcends the fleeting youth,
In between beats where hearts are bowed.

Seconds stretch to fill the void,
Between the beats, love's silence thrives.
In those moments we're employed,
To see how deeply love survives.

In the gaps, emotions teem,
Life and love, in whispers meet.
In between beats, we find the dream,
And in that space, our hearts complete.

www.ingramcontent.com/pod-product-compliance
Lightning Source LLC
LaVergne TN
LVHW010555070526
838199LV00063BA/4982